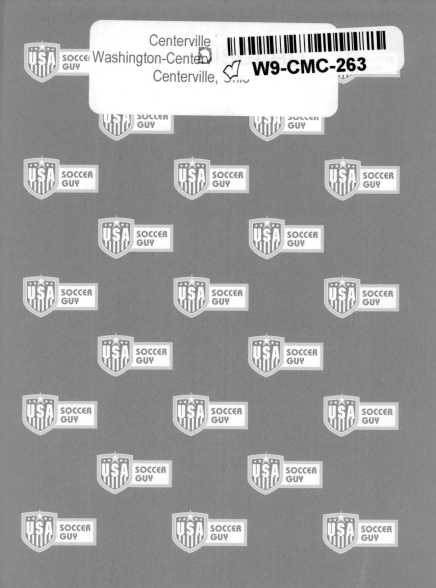

USA SOCCER GUY'S

50 INSANE SOCCER MOMENTS

PORTICO

CONTENTS

1 Ross takes a death-strike 008

2 Old Ladies take a fall 009

3 The Hand-Felony of God 010

4 Buyatelly celebrates 4 July at home 012

9 Qatar wins a World Cup 022

10 Terry Henry thwarts luck of the Irish 024

11 Abou Diaby royal family buys a Manchester franchise 028

15 Liver Pool make it back from the dead 036

16 Cantuna kicks a soccer fan 040

17 Rivaldo acts like a total douchebag 04

21 Scotland win against nobody 052

22 Cheerleader gets a cleat-rocket in the face 053

23 Terry John misses the deathstrike 054

27 Swearez takes a bite 064

28 Ahn knocks out Italy 068

29 Dogbra wins it with his last kick 070

33 Gazza cries tears of soccer sadness 074

34 Graham Pole is bad at math 078

35 O'Carlos scores a felony kick 079

39 Landon Donovan wears a sports bra 090

40 Espíndola in foot fracture felony 091

41 Scorpion hand denial 092

45 Adu has a tryout for the Unity 101

46 Ramos drops a soccer cup 104

47 The Crazy Guys win the England Soccer Cup 10

5 Zidane head-kicks some guy **016**

6 Di Caprio pushes over a referee **018**

7 Raiders get kicked out **020**

8 Beckham steps up **021**

12 Zaire felony kick deefense **030**

13 Ibrahimovic buys Chelsea **031**

14 Gobbler feeds spaghetti to Italians **034**

18 Madonna fails a drug test **044**

19 Figo and the pig's head **046**

20 "Soccer – Bloody Hell!" **050**

24 Green's hand-denial fail **058**

25 Pedalo Mendes 'scores' **062**

26 McClaren goes Scandinavian **063**

30 Leeds Union, relegationized **071**

31 Beckham gets a cleat in the face **072**

32 Hand felony hurts Africa **073**

36 Special Juan announces himself **080**

37 This is soccer, not a hockey match **082**

38 Robert O'Baggio's deathstrike fail **086**

42 Schumacher KOs a French guy **093**

43 Agwearooooo oooooooooo **098**

44 Denial-flag heartache for USMNT **100**

48 Geoff Hurts 'scores' a goalshot **106**

49 Kuwait here a minute, guys **108**

50 Zico goalshot denied by completion whistle **110**

HEY.

Popularity is a pretty crazy thing, right? I mean, take a look at the great singers and songwriters of the last century and you'll maybe get where I'm coming from: Michael Jackson, Madonna, Elvis Presley, John Lennon, Ja Rule, Elton John … Did you ever take a look at these guys and ask yourself how they got to be so popular?

I sure did. The more I thought about it, the answer was kinda easy. You gotta be in the right place at the right time. No matter how much talent those guys have, if they aren't on the right platform, then that talent is totally wasted.

Before you guys that thought you were getting a book on soccer get all weirded out, let me just say that I'm getting to my point.

I am Soccer Guy. I am American. I have a passion for the sport of soccer that goes back further than most. Way back to the summer of '94, to be accurate. That was the summer when the sport was truly globalized right the way around the globe, thanks to my country getting to host the World Soccer Cup.

The dominance of the Alexi Lalas-led US Men's National Soccer Team (USMNT) was a pretty obvious attraction—but there was more to it than that. I loved the uniforms, the fact that there was only one time-out, the way that there were only two quarters instead of four and, despite all the pretty obvious differences, the way that some European guys thought it was like football.

Here was a sport that was clearly not that popular, but still all kinds of different countries were tryin' real hard to play it.

Thanks to that summer, the lives of many were changed into way better, soccer-filled ones. As it has done with most things, the USA had shown the way for the rest of mankind. After years of trying, everyone could now take this sport to their hearts.

The '94 World Soccer Cup in America was therefore the sport's platform to popularity. My own platform would come almost twenty years later.

The excitement of soccer was burning inside me, and I started to read around. Amazingly, I discovered that many places right around the world had already been playing the sport for a long time. Places in Europe had establishized pretty lame leagues that could not even afford cheerleaders.

When the internet came along, I found it even easier to find out cool stuff about the history of soccer, and by the turn of the millennium I was pretty much fluent in soccer speak. Being recognized for my depth of soccer knowledge was surely not too far away.

Actually, things started to happen around my spring break, 2013. I created my own Twitter page (@usasoccerguy), to get my voice heard. Specializing in the developments of the English EPL League, my views on soccer in Europe soon drew some attention.

My follower count got pretty big, and I soon found myself being congratulized by soccer lovers right the way around the globe. Having chosen a picture of Alexi Lalas as my Twitter page picture, I was honored when the man himself began to follow just a few weeks after I launched.

By the time fall came around, I had hit the big time. After years of loving soccer I had become one of the most powerful voices within the sport.

So I guess getting asked to write a book was pretty much expected. Sure, I am honored, but it's not so much of a big deal. It's kinda expected. Like I said at the start of this: if you got the talent, all you gotta do is find that platform. I found it.

A look at some of soccer's most insane moments through American eyes is something that hasn't really been done before—go check the bookstore. Having just notched up another World Soccer Cup, a book that does this is nodoubtedly overdue.

Soccer is way more than just the goalshots, and this book will hopefully show this, ranging from the real famous moments—like major felony cards in World Soccer Cup finals and Landon Donovan wearing a sports bra—to lesser known events like some German cheerleader unexpectedly getting a cleat-rocket right in her face.

So go right ahead! Enjoy the read as you educize yourself on some of the weirdest events to take place on and around the soccer field.

DIANA ROSS TAKES A REAL BAD DEATHSTRIKE

The opening ceremony of the greatest World Soccer Cup the world has ever seen was one of the high points in soccer history. It is widely known by many as the day that soccer really started. The organizers were clearly pretty smart guys and, realizing that nothing screams 'World Soccer Cup' more than a Motown diva, they invited Diana Ross along to join the party.

Singing some song, the climax would be when Ross ran up to a soccer ball and kicked it real hard into the soccer net past a helpless goaltender. Then, the goal would fall apart and she'd run through it and go someplace else, making a truly *supreme* spectacle in front of the eyes of the watching world.

The problem was, Diana Ross is not a soccer player. Her deathstrike technique was bad, and she wound up kicking the sphere of leather way wide of the soccer goal. Even if the goaltender had been trying to *reach out and touch* the soccer ball, he would have got nowhere near it. This sparked a *chain reaction* of laughter right around the world and turned Diana Ross' love for all things soccer well and truly *upside down*.

Nevertheless, the party had started.

THE OLD LADIES TAKE A FALL

>> TURIN, ITALY, 2006

In their black and white striped uniform, Juventus Soccer Franchise is one of the world's most recognizable soccer franchises. With humongous support around Italy, life seemed pretty good for the Old Ladies back in the mid-'00s. At the end of the '06 soccer season, they'd just become Serious A World Champions again. But the 'Old Ladies', as they are known, were about to have one humongous fall. Reports hit the press that one of the Juventus director guys had tried to organize which soccer referees refereed soccer in their soccer matches. A serious felony in soccer, if the reports were true.

Juventus were kicked outta Serious A and the Euro Soccer Cup, and had to lose a whole bunch of awesome soccer players in the next franchise-enhancement window. Other franchises were also charged with some bad stuff, but it was Juventus that were in the biggest trouble.

The timing of this scandal kinda sucked for Italy as a soccer nation too. 2006 was the year that they just won the World Soccer Cup, but this pretty embarrassing situation meant that nobody really cared.

THE HAND
FELONY OF GOD

In the '80s, the sport of soccer was still years away from achieving the popularity boost that was the 1994 World Soccer Cup in the United States of America. The Mexican World Soccer Cup took place in Mexico in 1986, and the quarter-finals saw England Soccer Club take on Argentina in the unimaginatively named Mexico City.

Diego Madonna was the world soccer MVP and, it being the mid-'80s, was not yet the guy who became fat and took drugs and stuff. The two different sides of Madonna were shown up by the two goalshots he inserted on this day.

After half time-out, the scores were still knotted at 0s. A kick-pass over a mixed-up English deefense line saw the soccer ball wind up heading toward the edge of the English danger box zone. The English goaltender rushed out to try to make the hand denial. Madonna's nose sniffed out a lotta stuff during his lifetime but, on this occasion, that guy's nose could only sniff a goalshot opportunity.

Seeing the charging goaltender, the hobbit-like genius ran toward the soccer ball. As the soccer ball bounced up real high into the hot Mexican air, Madonna jumped up like some kinda fish in an Alaskan stream. Being real small, it would have been literally impossible for Madonna to issue the headkick and knowing this, he reached out an arm and kicked the ball with his hand and over the goaltender. Into the soccer goal interior it went.

Off the little guy went, clapping high fives to his buddies and hollering with total soccer joy. On the other hand, the English were pretty pissed at this and went insane at the soccer referee. Despite them being real mad, the goalshot was permitted.

After his felony-drenched first, Madonna added another less memorable goalshot. He took the soccer ball some place in the middle sector of the soccer field and ran past a load of deefense players before inserting. This was a way better goalshot, so the English guys probably didn't mind so much.

Toward the completion whistle, some guy who went on to famously advertize potato chips pulled one back. The score finished 2 to 1 at the completion whistle: the English were out, and the Argentinish were through.

The 'Hand Felony of God', as it would later be known, was a pretty important moment. It helped Madonna and his buddies as they went on to win the World Soccer Cup.

BUYATELLY CELEBRATES 4 JULY AT HOME

Mario Buyatelly. With his constantly changing hair and whacky clothes, the Italian guy is undeniafiably one of the most talked-about athletes on planet soccer. His career could probably provide enough stuff to fill this book all by itself!

Before he headed back home to Italy, Buyatelly had a coupla years playing for the Manchester City Sky Blues franchise in the English EPL League. His time there is fondly remembered by British soccer fans for a number of reasons, from great soccer kicks to bust-ups at soccer practice.

But one week in particular stands out from Mario's English adventure. After inviting a few of his buddies over to his place, reports broke that Mario had decided it'd be pretty cool to go let off some fireworks in his bathroom. He went right ahead and did this and, sure enough, a fire broke out in his house. Within an hour a fire truck from the MCFD had to be called out to stop the whole place burning to the ground!

After reports of this made the news, many expected Mario to start the next weekend's eagley anticipized Manchester Derby soccer match from the sub shack (if he was to make the roster at all). To the surprise of a load of guys, Coach Mankini gave Buyatelly a slot in the start-out line-up. The decision paid off pretty good for the City soccer coach too, as it was Buyatelly who opened up the goalshot tally that day as the Full Mooners crushed cross-town franchise the Manchester Unity 6 to 1 in their own soccer field. After inserting the soccer ball into the soccer goal interior, Mario lifted his soccer jersey to reveal a shirt underneath with a message reading 'WHY ALWAYS ME?'

After a pretty messed-up week, Buyatelly's goalshot and celebration were undeniafiably the greatest moments of his time in England.

The Nude Camp Barcelonia, Spain

Having no roof makes it look naked, hence the name.

THE SOCCER FIELD

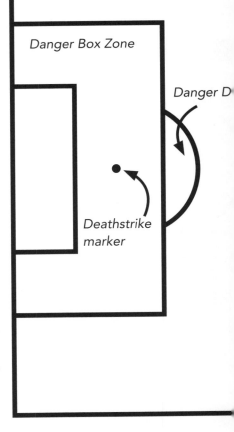

Sub shack

Danger Box Zone

Danger D

Deathstrike marker

The Soccer Field A pretty big rectangle of grass, approximately the same size as a football field, where soccer is played.

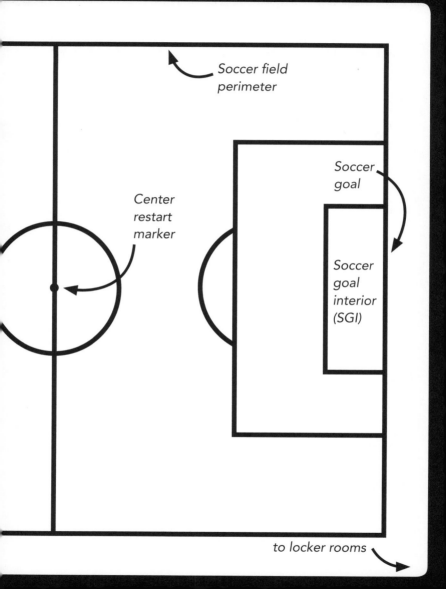

Soccer field perimeter

Soccer goal

Center restart marker

Soccer goal interior (SGI)

to locker rooms

ZIDANE HEADKICKS SOME GUY

As far as soccer heads go, Zidenine Zidane had one of the most famous. It had already kicked in two outta the three goals for France Soccer Club in their 1998 World Soccer Cup final victory.

But when the French reached another World Soccer Cup final in 2006, it was famous for all the wrong reasons.

In the German city of Berlin, Germany, the scores were all tied up at ones with the soccer in the World Soccer Cup between France and Italy. The game was headed to a Deathstrike Showdown.

The two guys that had already scored that night were Zidane for the French and deefense guy Maserati for the Italians. Reports suggested that Maserati had been a total douchebag to Zidane all night, constantly grabbing a hold of his jersey.

Having tolerized it for most of the soccer match, Zidane had gotten pretty mad by this stage. A conversation took place between the two athletes on the edge of the Italian DBZ. Some made allegations that Maserati said some real bad stuff about Zidane's mom, but even after several years, these alligators have never been proven right. Although the precise words have never been confirmed, it probably went a little something like this:

Zidane: 'Hey, quit grabbing my soccer jersey already!'

Maserati: 'Quit whining, you humongous douchebag.'

If Zidane was Bruce Banner he woulda probably turned green and his soccer uniform would have ripped off or something. Zidane is not Bruce Banner, but he still got crazy, turning round and kicking Maserati real hard with his head. Maserati fell to the ground like he'd just been hit by a freight train, and Zidane was issued with the major felony card.

This was a super-sized blow for the French, who went on to lose the soccer match on deathstrikes. Zidane had gone from being a French national hero all around the world to being a guy everyone was mad at.

Pictures sure do say a lotta words: the photograph of Zidane, looking sadder than the end of *Marley and Me* as he headed past the World Soccer Cup Cup and back to the locker room is one of the most famous ever taken in the soccer world. Ashamed by his actions, he never played soccer again. With one kick with his head, the completion whistle had been blown on one of the game's all-time MVPs.

DI CAPRIO PUSHES OVER A SOCCER REFEREE

Paolo Di Caprio was an EPL favourite in the late '90s and early '00s, representing the franchises of Sheffield Midweekers, Westside Hammers and the Charleston Athletes.

His style of soccer was great and he was undeniafiably one of the EPL's stars during his stay in England. But there were moments of drama too.

Di Caprio is famously remembered for what happened this one time he was playing a soccer match at the hump-day-named franchise from Sheffield. A hockey-style fight broke out on the soccer field between the Midweekers players and players from their opponents that day, London Arsenal. After the whole thing cooled down a little, Di Caprio was taken to one side and given a major felony card by the soccer referee.

Things were already pretty bad for the fired-up Italian, but they were about to get way worse. Totally mad at the decision, Di Caprio grabbed a hold of the soccer referee and pushed the guy down to the grass-covered field. Off he went to take a shower. This was the last that was seen of Di Caprio for a real long time.

But this story does have some kinda happy ending. A couple of years later—once Di Caprio had moved on to Westside Hammers in London and had not pushed any more soccer referees over—in a soccer match with Evertown, Di Caprio was given the chance to make the score into the Soccer Candies' net. To the shock of everybody in the Goodison Candy Shack Soccer Park that day, Di Caprio picked up the soccer ball with his hands and pointed to some Evertown guy that had got hurt on the floor.

After being shown as a total soccer douche for the soccer-referee push only a couple of years before, Paolo Di Caprio had learnt from his misdemeanor and shown that he was a pretty nice guy after all.

GLASGOW RAIDERS GET KICKED OUT OF EPL SCOTLAND

>> GLASGOW, SCOTCHLAND, 2012

Glasgow Raiders were kicked outta the Scotch EPL in 2012, breaking the hearts of Scotch soccer fans everywhere. After having no money, the decision was made to send the Raiders to some lame league.

The impact on the city of Glasgow was pretty big. The Raiders are one of few Scotch franchises that people have heard of, and this meant that the cross-town franchise, The Celtics (the Boston Celtics' Scotch soccer franchise) would not be able to do soccer in the eagley anticipized Old Friends derby for a real long time.

The Raiders sure were mad, but there was nothing that the Ibronx franchise could do except lace up those soccer cleats, dust off their soccer uniforms and go get some wins. And that is what they've been trying to do ever since.

BECKHAM MAKES THE STEP UP

Looking at the megastar that David Beckham has become, it's hard to imagine that he actually played soccer way before moving to California. This was the peak of his soccer career as he arrived Stateside to sign up to the Los Angeles Galaxy in Major League Soccer.

Not many remember Beckham's soccer career pre-LA, but he had already represented Manchester Unity and Real Salt Lake's Spanish-based Madrid franchise before he made the switch to the Los Angeles Galaxy, and 'Goalshot Balls' excited soccer fans right around the world as he got off the airplane at LAX.

'Goalshot Balls', as he had become known, was lethal with his felony kicks and was well known for accurately kicking his accurate cross-pass kicks with real accuracy. He continued to do nice soccer in the States, and even got his hands on the MLS cup—his finest soccer moment.

Since hanging up his cleats in 2013, Beckham has turned his attention to starting out his own MLS franchise. Confirmization that this will be in Miami, FL, has also been made.

QATAR WINS THE RIGHT TO HOST A WORLD SOCCER CUP

>> ZURICH, SWITZERLAND, 2010

Previous hosts of the World Soccer Cup have always had at least one of a couple of things in common:

1 **They are pretty awesome at the sport (USA, Brazil, Germany, Italy, Spain)**

Or

2 **They are crazy for it (England, Mexico)**

With those two things in mind, then, World Soccer President Seth Blatter and his buddies shocked the world in 2010 when he decided to award the 2022 competition to a place called 'Qatar', rejecting the opportunity to take the tournament back to the United States of America, where the standard was set for the tournament in 1994.

Although it is officially recognized as a real country, Qatar is real small and is situated in the middle of a real hot desert. It did not seem like the smartest of ideas to give a summertime tournament to a country that is as hot as a

McDonald's grill. Added to that, very few of the very few people that live there actually do soccer, so it kind of left a few people scratching their heads about why the World Soccer Cup was headed there.

Whatever the reasons to award this ridiculously hot, desert-covered, small, unpopulated, oil-rich country the greatest sports tournament in the world, the decision stands. It sure sounds great.

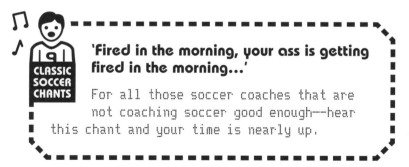

CLASSIC SOCCER CHANTS

'Fired in the morning, your ass is getting fired in the morning...'

For all those soccer coaches that are not coaching soccer good enough—hear this chant and your time is nearly up.

TERRY HENRY THWARTS LUCK OF THE IRISH

>> PARIS, FRANCE, 2009

Paris is a city that is probably most famous for being the European home of Mickey Mouse. But what took place there in this soccer match in 2009 was definitely no Disney fairytale.

With a place at the 2010 World Soccer Cup up for grabs, Ireland Soccer Club had to face off against the big-time favorites of France.

BEST EURO FRANCHISES

Barcelonia

Approximately one half of the two biggest Spanish franchises, Barcelonia have totally owned European soccer in recent years with their tippy-tappy soccer play. They have been drawing the big crowds to their Nude Camp stadium for centuries, and have an awesome roster at their disposal.

Terry Henry was one of the game's megastars. Having scored goalshots by the truckload for London Arsenal, Henry had left the Soccer Cannons for Barcelonia in EPL Spain, where his soccer would ultimately gain him a move to the big time with the New York Red Bulls.

With the game tied up and heading for deathstrikes, the soccer ball reached Henry in the Irish danger box zone. Henry struggled to get that soccer ball under control and, as it headed outta play, he kicked it away from the perimeter line with his hand, before making a pass-kick to some other French guy, who inserted it into the SGI!

The soccer referee did not see the hand felony, and the goalshot was allowed. Unfortunately for the Irish, it was to be the only one of the soccer match, leaving them looking like a bunch of wolf cubs that just watched some real mean guy cut off their mom's head with an axe.

Goalshot What soccer is all about. If your franchise is gonna win at soccer they gotta score more goalshots than their opponents.

ABOU DIABY ROYAL FAMILY BUYS A MANCHESTER FRANCHISE

Back in 2008, the English city of Manchester, England, was already pretty famous on the soccer scene. Along with rock band The Beatles, Manchester was also host to the Manchester Unity—world famous throughout the world for being one of the most trophied soccer franchises in existence.

That summer, the Manchester soccer skyline was about to change forever. A few blocks away from the Unity's Old Trafford Center soccer stadium, you find the city's other franchise—Manchester City. Famous for being pretty lame compared to their red-uniformed cross-town buddies, the guys from the City of Manchester Soccer Park were spectacularly bought out by the Abou Diaby royal family, instantly transforming them into one of the richest sports franchises in the world of sport.

The new owners quickly spent the dollars on a roster overhaul, and the soccer franchise became pretty awesome, prompting the Unity's Coach Ferguson to name them the 'real loud neighbors'. The years that have followed the Abou Diaby buyout have been pretty cool for the fans of this soccer franchise. 2011 saw them end their trophy famine as they beat Stoked City at the Wembley Arena to win the England Franchise Association Cup. Better was to follow as the guys claimed their first EPL World Championship in a real long time in dramatic style in 2012.

Wembley Arena, London, England

Sometimes called the 'home of football', despite only hosting a few NFL games in its history.

ZAIRE FELONY KICK DEEFENSE

Zaire were clearly pumped to be doing their soccer at the 1974 World Soccer Cup. But when defending a dangerous felony kick against Brazil Soccer Club, they were way *too* pumped.

As the Salsa Boys put the soccer ball down, the referee blew the whistle to start the play. Before the Brazilians had chance to even move, some asshat from Zaire ran real quick and kicked the soccer ball right the way to the other end of the soccer field.

Not knowing the rules of soccer, the African guy must have felt like a complete douchebag. This was a felony that would be punishable with a minor offense card as the Brazilians took the victory points in an easy 3 to 0 victory.

Although he did look stupid, the guy later claimed that he had been trying to get the major felony card in protest at not being paid by the Zaire.

IBRAHIMOVIC BUYS CHELSEA

>> LONDON, ENGLAND, 2003

London, England—home to the Queen. In 2003, one of the richest guys in Russia decided to make her one of his neighbors when he splashed out on buying a soccer franchise.

Chelsea Franchise Club were Roman Ibrahimovic's choice, and his purchase would change the face of the EPL League forever. At the time, the franchise named were not that great, although they had managed to make it into the playoffs for the Euro Soccer Cup.

Almost immediately Ibrahimovic started to buy way better players for the blue guys and let some of the lamer soccer players go off someplace else. It was the ultimate franchise-enhancement window as international soccer legends such as Hermán Crespo and Ron Geremi walked through the doors of Stanford Bridge.

The free-spending franchise soon turned out to be one of the winningest, too, claiming back-to-back EPL World Championships in 2005 and 2006 for the first time in fifty years.

TOP 10 FELONY KICK SPECIALISTS

10 Robert O'Carlos
The little Brazilian with supersized thighs kicked soccer balls real hard throughout his soccer career.

9 Didier Dogbra
The African was as awesome at making a score from a felony kick as he was from winning them.

>>>

8 Cristiarnold Ronaldo
The Portugaleze kicks ass when it comes to kicking felony kicks into the soccer goal interior.

>>>

7 Andreas Pearlo
The felony kicks of this Italian guy are as artistic as one of Mozart's paintings.

6 Stevie Gee
The guy from Mercy town has racked a whole bunch of great felony kicks for Liver Pool and England Soccer Club.

Some soccer players have made a name for themselves by being able to kick a soccer ball into the net directly from a felony kick. Here are ten of the best.

5 Iron Robben
What this guy lacks in hair he makes up for in felony kick ability.

>>

4 RSVP
Another Dutch guy, RSVP can punish any franchise with one flash of that left cleat.

3 David Beckham
The former British captain perfected his felony kick when he arrived in the MLS.

>>>>>>>>>>>>>>>>>>>>>>>>>> >>>>>>>>>>>>>>>>>>>>>>>>>>

2 Junhinho
After playing in the EPL way back for Middlesberg, the Brazilian went on to be one of the most successful felony kick strikers in the world for the Olympic Lyon Franchise in EPL France.

1 Clint Dempsey
A soccer player so good that he doesn't even need to take felony kicks that much.

>>

BRUCE GOBBLER FEEDS SPAGHETTI TO THE ITALIAN GUYS

Back in 1984, the Euro Soccer Cup was hosted in the Italian city of Rome. Despite being home to the oldest soccer stadium in the world, the Colosseum, the soccer match was played in some other place.

As is usually the case, two franchises would face off for the Cup that night. Liver Pool of England had travelled to Rome on a quest to go win their fourth Euro Soccer Cup. Their opponent franchise had not had to travel that far. Rome Franchise Club—actually from Rome—were doing soccer on their own soccer field. Playing in their home town was not the advantage that the Rome guys would have thought. To be fair, the soccer match was pretty bad and ended—like a lot of soccer finals tend to—knotted up.

With each franchise scoring one goalshot each, for the first time in the history of soccer history, the Euro Soccer Cup final would be decided on a deathstrike showdown. After a few guys scored, some other guys did not—but this soccer match will be remembered for the actions of the Liver Pool goaltender, Bruce Gobbler.

Inspirized by Italian food, Gobbler started goofing around when one of the Italian guys was about to do his deathstrike, pretending his legs were made outta spaghetti and that he was real scared.

Although pretty funny to watch, this was an attempt to totally psych out the Italian guy...and it sure did work! He kicked that soccer ball real hard and way over the pipes. The following deathstrike was inserted by one of Gobbler's buddies, and Liver Pool had their hands on the Euro Soccer Cup again.

Liver Pool would wait over twenty years to go win another ESC, and the actions of Gobbler would also play a part that night too.

LIVER POOL MAKE IT BACK FROM THE DEAD

Soccer, they say, is a game of two quarters. Never before has this quirky little phrase been more appropriate.

Finishing behind Mercy Town rivals Evertown in the EPL League, 2005 had pretty much sucked for the red-uniformed Liver Pool. A consolization was that they had made it all the way to the Euro Soccer Cup, where they would face Italian franchise Ace Milan in what those European guys call the 'Super Bowl of Soccer'.

What happened in the first quarter of the game was kinda like watching your pet dog get run over by a monster truck. Old guy Paul O'Maldini and Hermán Crespo had been like soccer artists painting some kind of real nice soccer masterpiece, leaving the guys with the Liver Duck on their franchise emblem 3–zip down as they headed into the locker rooms for half time-out.

But, when a Stevie Gee headkick found its way into the score net, a totally insane six minutes of soccer were about to get played.

A few minutes later, some other guy did a kick from real far out. The Brazilian goaltender looked like he was gonna just pick the soccer ball up but, after a major hand fail, the soccer ball got into the soccer goal interior once again. Outta nowhere, the English were right back in the soccer match at 3 to 2.

Right after that, Liver Pool got the soccer ball back and made yet another offensive play on the Ace's danger box zone. A mistimed depossession slide brought down Stevie Gee and a deathstrike was awarded. Spanish guy Chavvy Alonso kicked it, but Dido made the hand denial...the soccer ball Rick O'Shead right back to Alonso who kicked it into the SGI. The equalization had been made.

After the comeback, Liver Pool took the soccer match through to a deathstrike showdown. After a bunch of fails for the Aces, Liver Pool took the victory, and the big shiny cup was lifted by Stevie Gee, as 'You Never Walk Away' got sung real loud by the happy fans.

Headkick A bodily movement done by the body where the soccer ball is kicked by the head. This can be done all over the soccer field and is best done when the soccer ball is in the air.

CANTUNA KICKS A SOCCER FAN

Before heading to England, Eric Cantuna was well known in France for being a little crazy. He had got in a couple of bust-ups with a few guys from his own franchise and, in one incident, ripped off his soccer jersey and kicked the soccer ball into the crowd when asked to head back to the sub shack. In the end, it was time for him to head to England, and he arrived at the Manchester Unity via Leeds Union.

Under the soccer coaching of Coach Ferguson, it appeared Cantuna had chilled out, and he was a humongous part of their success in the '94 EPL World Championship and Franchise Association Cup victories.

Fast forward a few months on from the end of that awesome Soccer Devil season, and Manchester Unity were looking to go win some more trophies as the '94–'95 season was heating up. This time it was the Blackburn Roosters that were heading for the EPL World Championship, but the Unity were right behind.

Eric Cantuna was the Unity's MVP, and things started going real bad for his franchise one January night in January 1995. After kicking some guy in a soccer match, Cantuna was issued with the major felony card. Already, this was bad news for him, but when a soccer fan in the crowd started shouting some mean stuff about Cantuna's mom, the Unity man went totally insane.

Having been walking to the locker room, Cantuna turned and walked toward the guy in the crowd and launched at him with his soccer cleat. Eventually the fight got broke up, but the soccer world was in total shock.

Cantuna wound up with a real long ban from the soccer field. It was a major loss for his franchise as the Unity lost out to the Roosters for the EPL World Championship.

Cantuna confused the hell out of everyone when he found out that he was banned from soccer for a real long time:

'Sometimes a bunch of seagulls go flying after a boat, they do this because they're probably pretty hungry and just want some sardines or something.'

What he said was probably true, but to this day, nobody knows why he even did that.

RIVALDO ACTS LIKE A TOTAL DOUCHEBAG

17

>> SAITAMA, JAPAN, 2002

One thing's for sure, it doesn't get any bigger than a World Soccer Cup semi-final. In 2002 Turkey were playing Brazil Soccer Club for a shot at making the final.

The Brazilian guys had one of the most winningest rosters at that soccer tournament, and one of their main stars was Barcelonia's talented Rivaldo.

A whole load of soccer talent does not always mean that you can't act like a jerk though—as Rivaldo would show. As he went to take a restart kick from the corner, some Turkish guy kicked the soccer ball to him, hitting him on the lower leg armor.

Instead of just taking the kick, Rivaldo fell over, holding his face like it just got hurt real bad! Amazingly, the soccer referee decided that the Turkey soccer player had done enough to receive that dreaded red major FC.

It sure looked like Rivaldo's douchebagism had contributized to a huge moment in this soccer match, and the Salsa Boys went on to claim the victory by the one goalshot. The next week, they also claimed victory in the final over Germany Soccer Club.

As Brazil triumphed, the country named after the great Thanksgiving bird sure were not thankful to one of the lamest acts ever witnessed in a World Soccer Cup soccer match.

BEST EURO FRANCHISES

Manchester City Franchise Club

One of the lamest franchises in EPL history until a few years back, the Abu Diaby owners have shot the Moon-lovin' team to the top of the Euro Soccer Cup money roster. They may still have a while to go before they equalize with the guys from a few blocks away, but the blue sector of Manchester, England is heading the right way right now.

MADONNA FAILS A DRUG TEST AT THE WORLD SOCCER CUP

Argentinish soccer hero Diego Madonna had singlehandedly seen off England Soccer Club *en route* to World Soccer Cup glory eight years before he arrived in the United States of America for the '94 tournament. By that time, he was not that great anymore.

A couple of years beforehand, he had already been banned from over a year of soccer after he tested positive for drug use—a far cry from the (legal) highs of his career in the Mexican World Soccer Cup.

Following his drug felonies and the fact that he was now pretty old, many doubters doubted Madonna's ability to do good soccer this time around. But the first two soccer matches showed that the little guy still knew how to kick a soccer ball real nice. He scored a goalshot in the first soccer match against Greece Soccer Club and also played in the second game against the African state of Nigeria.

The celebration that followed his goalshot in the first match showed that he was still addicted to the sport of soccer: yelling real loud, Madonna ran straight toward the TV cameras, staring like a crazy guy with bulging eyes into the lens. Following such a joyful celebration, it came as a real shock to the soccer world when the World Soccer Cup Dope Squad chose to 'randomly' test Madonna after the Nigeria match.

Sure enough, Madonna's pee showed that he tested positive for banned substances that came from some flu medication he had been taking. A second pee check also confirmed this, and Madonna's World Soccer Cup career came to an end one soccer match short of a record.

Colosseum
Rome, Italy

One of the oldest soccer stadiums in the world. Needs a refurb.

FIGO AND THE PIG'S HEAD

The rivalry between Real Madrid Franchise Club and Barcelonia is one of the most humongous in world soccer, let alone EPL Spain—those guys are always hatin' on each other.

One incident in 2002 totally weirded out the entire soccer world. The guy at the center of it all was the Portugaleze soccer sensation Lewis Figo. In the most recent franchise-enhancement window, Figo had made the switch from Barcelonia to Real Salt Lake's Madrid-based franchise.

BEST EURO FRANCHISES

Bryan Munich

The biggest soccer franchise in Germany are the guys from the Alienz arena, Munich. And man, do they play soccer from out of this world! Winners of a load of Euro Soccer Cups, many are kinda weirded out that they named themselves after a guy's name.

With the rivalry already hyped up enough, you don't have to be Frankenstein to work out that the Barcelonians were pissed when he returned to the Nude Camp wearing the all-white uniforms of the guys from the San Diego Bernabowl.

Aside from the Barcelonia fans singing in Mexican about what a jerk they thought he was, Figo had to put up with a whole bunch of crazy objects being thrown at him. Most insane of all was the head of a pig, when Figo was all set to take a restart kick from the corner.

The picture of the pig's head lying on the soccer field was beamed right the way round the world, and drew a lot of attention. How the Barcelonia fans managed to get an entire pig into a soccer stadium is one thing, but then to cut the animal's head off and throw it at a soccer player is another.

The trend of throwing animals' heads at soccer players you don't like never really took off, but this was indisputafiably one of the grossest things ever seen within the sport.

. . . . *HAND*

Hand denial The goaltender is the only soccer player allowed to use their hands to kick the ball without causing a felony, and a hand denial is where they deny a goalshot opportunity with their hands or other parts of their body.

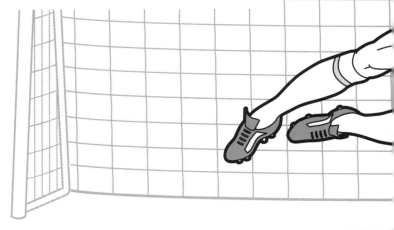

DENIAL

Trailing in the Euro Soccer Cup final of '99, Manchester Unity sent Terry Sheringham and Ollie Gonna Solskjaer outta the sub shack to try to turn it around against Bryan Munich in Barcelonia.

The Unity's German opposition had taken the lead earlier in the soccer match thanks to a real nice felony kick. The score had remained 1–zip as the overtime verdict tablet had been erected, and the Unity looked like they were never gonna score a goalshot. The three minutes of soccer that followed were three of the most insane moments in the history of soccer.

From a corner restart kick, Beckham kicked the soccer ball into the danger box zone and, after the Germans failed to make the box evacuation kick, Terry Sheringham wrapped his soccer cleat around the soccer ball and sent it in the soccer goal interior. The equalization had been made and the red sector of the Nude Camp went crazy… but the Unity were not finished there.

Straight after the restart, the Unity went forward again, and a corner restart cross-pass was awarded. Beckham once more kicked the soccer ball real high into the Barcelonia air. As it entered the DBZ, it was headkicked toward the soccer goal by Terry Sheringham once more. As the German deefense were as still as a moose that had been shot in the face by some guys on a hunting trip, Solskjaer pounced and kicked it real nice into the soccer goal interior.

As the completion whistle blew, the German guys started crying like a bunch of dumbass babies. The Unity fans and soccer players went crazy. History was made, as the Soccer Devils added their Euro Soccer Cup to their EPL Cup and English Soccer Cup they already had back home.

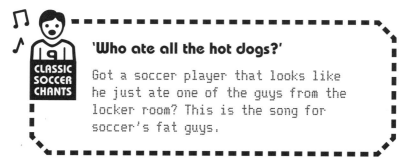

'Who ate all the hot dogs?'

Got a soccer player that looks like he just ate one of the guys from the locker room? This is the song for soccer's fat guys.

CLASSIC SOCCER CHANTS

SCOTLAND SOCCER CLUB WIN AGAINST NOBODY

>> SOMEPLACE CALLED ESTONIA, 1996

With the World Soccer Cup of 1998 on the horizon, the Soccer Nessies made a road trip to a place called 'Estonia' with their eyes on the victory points. But what greeted them was not what they expected.

After having soccer practice in the stadium where their match would be played, the Scotch were not happy with the lights that were supposed to illuminize the soccer field. After getting all grouchy about this, the soccer match unleashment whistle was moved from a sundown soccer time to an afternoon time where everyone could see real good. That kinda makes sense, right?

Wrong. The Estionish people were real mad at this and decided not to even turn out for the soccer match, leaving Scotland Soccer Club with the easiest soccer match they had ever done. The soccer match was played for just a few seconds before the referee realized it was a pretty dumb idea. The Scotch were awarded a 3–0 victory, which helped them make it to the France World Soccer Cup.

CHEERLEADER GETS A CLEAT-ROCKET IN THE FACE

When most people think of soccer, cheerleaders are probably one of the first things they think about. They are something that has always been there, and pretty much always will be.

Although they undeniafiably bring something to the soccer matches that just wouldn't be there without them, this incident must have left this girl wishing she'd stayed home.

Wolfsburg Franchise Club was already 3–zip up in their EPL Germany soccer match when one of their guys tried to kick the soccer ball into the soccer goal interior one more time. The soccer ball flew way over the pipes and smashed the cheerleader right in her face.

Luckily she wasn't hurt too bad, but the video footage became one of the most watched soccer clips on YouTube.

Since arriving in London, England, it was no secret that Roman Ibrahimovic wanted to transformize his blue-uniformed soccer franchise into one of the best in the world. They had never reached a Euro Soccer Cup final in their history, but the new additions to their roster made them way better.

After winning the EPL a couple of times under the coaching of Coach Juan Mourinho the guys came close, but when the Special Juan quit in 2007 it seemed like any Euro Soccer Cup glory was on the rocks.

With Janitor Coach Grant taking over the soccer practices, Chelsea Franchise Club surprised many when they made it right the way to the Euro Soccer Cup Final of 2008. The game would be played back in Mr Ibrahimovic's hometown of Moscow, Russia, against fellow EPL franchise the Manchester Unity.

After all the hype, the soccer match had finished all tied up at ones, and would be settled by a deathstrike showdown. In the last few minutes of the extra overtime, Didier Dogbra had been given the major felony card, which meant that one of the best deathstrike kickers on the Chelsea roster would not be taking one. Amazingly, the Unity's Cristiarnold Ronaldo was the first guy to make a deathstrike fail. When a couple more deathstrikes were successfully kicked into the SGI, it left Terry John with one kick to win that Cup.

Terry John was the on-field leader of Chelsea Franchise Club, and suddenly faced off with the most important kick of a soccer ball he had ever faced.

Rain had been falling on Moscow pretty much right the way through the soccer match, making the soccer field pretty slippy. As he stepped up to strike, his standing cleat slipped as his other made contact with the soccer ball, and although he sent the goaltender the total wrong way, the soccer ball hit the frame and Rick O'Shead behind. The chance to win that Cup had been washed away in the Moscow wetness.

This deathstrike fail would prove to be crucial for Roman Ibrahimovic's guys, as the Unity managed to insert all their remaining ones and Knickerless Anelka went and failed his too—allowing the Unity to take their third European World Championship.

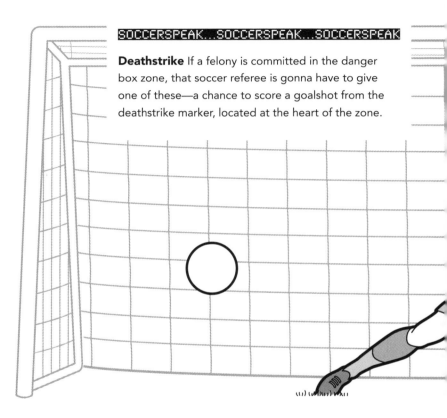

Deathstrike If a felony is committed in the danger box zone, that soccer referee is gonna have to give one of these—a chance to score a goalshot from the deathstrike marker, located at the heart of the zone.

DEATHSTRIKE!

ROBBIE GREEN'S HAND-DENIAL FAIL

Having made it all the way to the World Soccer Cup of 2010, England Soccer Club were dealt a real cruel blow when they had to play the United States of America in their first soccer match of the series.

Against all the odds, the English took a lead thanks to a Stevie Gee goalshot. That in itself was a humongous achievement for the 'Three Lines', who went about trying to hang on to their lead.

Unfortunately for the British, they could not hold back the soccering superiority of their American opponents. Their deefense held out until just before half time-out when the equalization was made by one of the players of that particular tournament, Clint Dempsey. The way that the soccer ball entered the soccer goal interior, however, left the English goaltender feeling like a bit of a dumbass.

Well known right around the soccer world for having a real powerful shot, Dempsey did not kick the soccer ball that hard, and it rolled real slow toward Robbie Green. With the simple task of picking the soccer ball up, Green made one of the most famous hand-denial fails ever made as the soccer ball slipped underneath him.

Amazingly, the English guys held on for a tie point. This proved to be crucial as they went on to make it outta the mini-league stage behind the USA—an awesome achievement. Despite it being a great achievement, it was kinda sad that one of their greatest victories ever was denied by a simple mistake.

Chelsea Franchise Club

BEST EURO FRANCHISES

Sure, the money of Roman Ibrahimovic has helped Chelsea Franchise Club. Following a few EPL League cups, a Euro Soccer Cup in 2012 added to this franchise's honors roster and has gone a long way toward making everyone think that 'Chelsea' is way more than Bill and Hillary Clinton's daughter.

TOP 10 GOALTENDERS

10 **Peter Smichaels**
One of the world's most awesome in his time at the Manchester Unity. His son, named after a friendly ghost, also is a goaltender.

9 **Oliver Khan**
Despite sounding like the Lion out of Jungle Book, this Khan was an angry-looking German guy who represented Bryan Munich in Germany.

>>>

8 **Iker Casius**
Starting out for Real Madrid when he was pretty young, the Spanish guy made his home between the pipes and was the captain for the victorious Spain Soccer Club in Africa 2010.

>>>

7 **Pete Cheque**
The Polish goaltender has become one of the world's best at Chelsea Franchise Club, and is instantly recognizable with his helmet.

6 **Eddie Vander Sar**
The big Scandinavian guy finished up a trophied career at the Manchester Unity after playing in Italy and for Ajax Soccer Franchise in his native Neverlands.

5 Gianluigi Buffet
Since moving to the Juventus franchise in Italy, soccer fans have been well fed on awesome goaltendering thanks to this Buffet. He also won the World Soccer Cup of 2006.

>>

4 Casey Keller
An American hero who denied the goalshots of thousands in EPL England for a short while before heading back to the MLS.

3 Brad Guzan
The latest off the production line of sparse-haired American goaltenders is Brad Guzan from Illinois. Playing for Ass Town Vanilla, he's already one of the greatest.

2 Tim Howard
After a brief spell at the Manchester Unity, T-Ho has totally owned it in Evertown.

>>

1 Brad Friedel
Real old. Real awesome. Brad Friedel still going strong.

>>

PEDALO MENDES 'SCORES' AT OLD TRAFFORD CENTER

When Totten Ham Whitespurs went to Manchester Unity's Old Trafford Center in 2005, they hadn't won a soccer match there in forever.

With the two franchises locked at 0s entering the later minutes of the second quarter, Portugaleze soccer player Pedalo Mendes decided he was gonna try to score a goalshot from his own defensive sector. Just near the half-sector line, Mendes kicked the soccer ball real hard toward the Unity soccer goal. It looked like a simple receive for the Unity goaltender, Ray Carroll, but that was not the case. He dropped it, and the soccer ball bounced back into the Unity SGI for what would surely hand the Soccer Chickens the victory points.

In desperation, Carroll threw himself over the SGI line and hooked the soccer ball back into play. As the Whitespurs fans went crazy with soccer joy, something kinda weird happened. The Unity continued to play soccer. Despite being an undeniafiable goalshot, the soccer referee and his helper guys did not see it. A real mad Totten Ham Whitespurs had to settle for the tie point, but it shoulda been all three.

McCLAREN GOES SCANDINAVIAN

Coach McClaren's failure to take England Soccer Club to some soccer tournament had already cost him his job. The picture of him holding an umbrella at the side of a soccer field had caused a bunch of newspapers to say real mean stuff about him.

Scared, he had fled to coach soccer in EPL Neverlands. Coach McClaren had not had time to learn the language in the new country he found himself coaching soccer in and, to make up for it, he decided to just speak his normal language, but in a Scandinavian accent like all the locals!

Once again, Coach Steve McClaren looked pretty dumb as the English got a hold of this. Videos of his new crazy accent racked up plenty of hits on YouTube and Coach Shteeve stayed away from Britain for a few more years.

SWEAREZ TAKES A BITE

>> LIVER POOL, ENGLAND, 2013

Despite being one of the most awesome kickers in the country, Swearez was not having the best of times in English soccer in 2013. After a bunch of other stuff had happened, he was already getting hated on by EPL League fans when Chelsea Franchise Club arrived at the Mercy Towners' soccer field in 2013.

When Chelsea deefense guy Branislav Abramovic got in his way, Swearez was seen grabbing a hold of his opponent's arm and taking a bite. The soccer referee missed it and, although Swearez did not get the major felony card, his actions got him banned from the soccer field for a real long time by the English Franchise Association.

This was not the first time that Swearez was guilty of an on-field bite felony, having already done so when playing for his last franchise in the Neverlands. Already famous for his real hard work rate, his decision to use his teeth was later affectionately named the soccer beaver by soccer fans right the way around the globe.

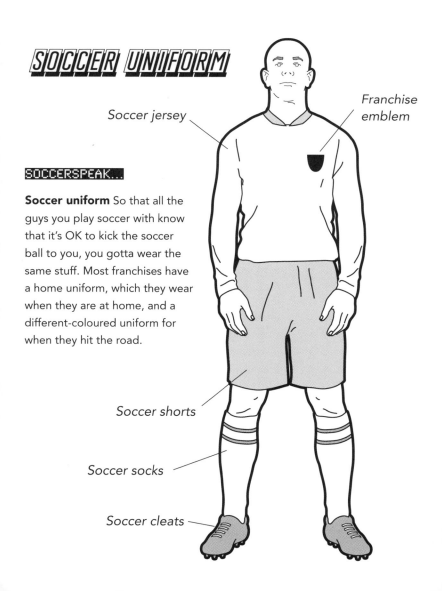

SOCCER UNIFORM

Soccer jersey

Franchise emblem

Soccer shorts

Soccer socks

Soccer cleats

TOP 10 WORST SOCCER UNIFORMS

10 **Cameroon Soccer Club, 2002**
Making a soccer jersey from a vest was pretty dumb. The Cameroonish guys looked like they were ready to go shoot some hoops with their sleeveless 2002 home uniform.

>>>

9 **Manchester Unity, 1995**
Making a gray uniform turned out to be a bad idea, as many soccer players could not even see each other when wearing it.

8 **London Arsenal, 1993**
This uniform of all yellow and black was totally gross and just looked like some guy had gotten sick on a bunch of soccer players to be mean.

>>>

7 **Hull City Franchise Club 1992–1993**
It might seem pretty cool to put a soccer franchise in a uniform made out of tiger skin, but it looked kinda wrong, and people were weirded out that a bunch of tigers got killed just to make some soccer jerseys.

6 **Mexican goaltender uniform, 1994**
Maybe this guy was trying to make the other soccer players blind or something. Why'd this guy get to design his kit?

Sometimes you gotta look the part on the soccer field, but these ten uniforms just made the guys in them look like a joke.

5 Bilbao Athletes, 2004
The EPL Spain franchise had uniforms that looked like somebody covered them in tomayto sauce.

4 Colorado Caribous
Before the MLS the Colorado franchise had their guys playing soccer in a uniform that had a frill right around it. It and they did not last.

>>>

3 Norwitch City 1994
The franchise with a yellow duck on their uniform looked like they got a load of ducks to go take a crap on their uniforms way back in 1994.

>>>

2 Newcastle Union 2009–2010
After hitting the EPL disaster sector back in 2009, the Soccer Skunks caused a real stink when they started to wear a yellow striped uniform.

1 Barcelonia 2012–2013
Even the world's most awesome franchises look pretty stupid at times. With an away jersey of bright yellow and orange, Barcelonia looked like they were headed to Guantanamo Bay jail.

AHN KNOCKS OUT ITALY

Before the times when the World Soccer President would give the World Soccer Cup to countries that had massive oil reserves, Seth Blatter and his buddies gave Japan and the part of Korea that is not always saying it's gonna go blow things up a shot at hosting.

The Korea Southsiders, as you'd expect from an Asian country, were not that good at soccer, normally. But the home advantage sure had helped them out as they made their way through the mini-leagues to face off against Italy Soccer Club in the super sixteens.

Although the USMNT's 2 to 0 victory a day earlier was the big story of the World Soccer Cup at the time, what happened that day turned a bunch of heads.

Soccer City, South Africa, Africa

Where the country of Africa saw its first World Cup final.

After leading through a Christian Vieira goalshot for most of the soccer match, the Italians already had to suffer the embarrassment of letting an Asian team tie things up late on, forcing the match into extra overtime. The golden goalshot law was in place, meaning that one mix-up in the deefense could be the end of their summer of soccer.

But it was not the Korean Southsiders that were about to go home. A cross-pass was headkicked into the Italian soccer goal interior by the head of a guy named Ahn. The Southsiders went crazy as a sea of soccer joy that got every guy in the entire country real wet.

Ironically, Ahn, the hero of the hour, was owned by some Italian franchise in Italy. This goalshot got the franchise owner pretty pissed and, real mad at what had happened, he fired Ahn's glorious Korean ass. He never set cleat on an Italian soccer field ever again.

DOGBRA WINS IT WITH HIS LAST KICK

>> MUNICH, GERMANY, 2012

The Euro Soccer Cup of 2012 was a special one for all Chelsea Franchise Club fans. After Terry John's famous miss four years earlier, this was the night that Roman Ibrahimovic's guys finally got their hands on that Cup.

Hosted in the German city of Munich in Germany, for the Blue Lions it looked like it was gonna be more heartache after they went behind to their opponents, hometown franchise Bryan Munich, pretty late on. After the overtime verdict board was erected, Didier Dogbra, in his farewell match in a blue uniform, headkicked the equalization goalshot.

Once again, the soccer match finished up with a deathstrike showdown. After a fail by a Bryan soccer player, it just so happened that with one kick, in his final soccer match in a blue uniform, Dogbra could win the Euro Soccer Cup.

Up he stepped and calmly inserted it into the SGI. The Bryan Munich fans, in their own Alienz Arena, were watching a soccer horror movie unfold before their German eyes.

As the African left Chelsea Franchise Club, Didier Dogbra, as his second name suggests, had a whole load of cups.

LEEDS UNION RELEGATIONIZED

When the new millennium started in approximately 2000, life seemed great for the soccer fans of Leeds Union, England. The Yorkshire state franchise were putting together a group of great soccer players and starting to look like the real deal: serious contenders for the EPL World Championship by 2001 and enjoying an awesome run in the Euro Soccer Cup, making it all the way to the semi-finals before losing.

To the horror of the Leeds soccer fans, this was as good as it got for their beloved franchise. After getting a few sums wrong, Leeds Union were losing money. Within a couple of years, they had to sell some of their better soccer players and found themselves staring at a battle to maintain their EPLism.

After losing a few soccer matches, Leeds Union, one of the biggest franchises in England, lost to Bowltown Wonders in the last round of matches in the 2004 EPL season. The defeat left them stuck in the EPL disaster sector with no escape. To this date, they have never returned to the English top league board.

BECKHAM GETS A CLEAT IN THE FACE

Little is said about Beckham's pre-Los Angeles Galaxy career. His years in Manchester, England, were probably the most trophied, but they also contained some controversial moments.

In 2003, Beckham's time in at the Manchester Unity was coming to an end. Rumours circulized that Coach Ferguson and Beckham now hated each other, and this incident did nothing to cool those stories.

On the field, the Unity's rivalry with London Arsenal was still going strong, and when the Soccer Cannons came to the Manchester Unity for an England Soccer Cup match in 2003 it did not go too great for Coach Ferguson. The Cannons fired their way to victory, sending the Unity outta the Cup.

Mad at this, a red-faced Coach Ferguson went crazy back in the locker room. In his fury, he kicked a soccer cleat real hard across the room. David Beckham's head was in the way and, as the cleat struck his head, it opened up a cut that no Band-Aid would fix.

When pictures hit the press of Beckham's gash, it seemed that his time in Manchester was pretty much done. Beckham was understandably real mad at this, and he quit the Old Trafford Center that summer for a few years in EPL Spain.

HAND FELONY HURTS AFRICA

>> SOUTH AFRICA, AFRICA, 2010

When it came to soccer, 2010 was an awesome one for Africa. It was the first time the country got to see the World Soccer Cup on their patch. After all the other African states had got ejected from the tournament, the entire country was behind the remaining state of Ghana, who played Uruguay.

Knotted at ones at the end of hyper-overtime, Uruguay Soccer Club's deefense was running scared like a bunch of penguins running away from a real hungry polar bear. When one of the Africans kicked the soccer ball past the goaltender, it looked like a definite goalshot.

Back on the soccer goal line was Lewis Swearez who, realizing that they were facing defeat, reached out his arm and kicked the soccer ball away with his hand. After denying what would have been the winning goalshot, Swearez's felony earned him the major felony card, and the Africans were one successful deathstrike away from the next round.

Unfortunately, the deathstrike failed and Swearez, still on his way to the locker room, celebrated at the side of the field. To make things a whole lot worse for Africa, Ghana went and lost out on the deathstrike showdown. Swearez's felonyful actions had played a humongous part in Uruguay Soccer Club's victory.

GAZZA CRIES TEARS OF SOCCER SADNESS

>> TURIN, ITALY, 1990

Usually, it's pretty funny when guys cry about soccer, but the tears of Paul Gascoin in Italy back in 1990 melted the hearts of even the meanest of soccer fans.

England Soccer Club had not started the 1990 World Soccer Cup too good, so it was surprizing to everyone when they found themselves making it all the way to the semi-finals against the Germany Westsiders.

The talents of Totten Ham Whitespur's 'Gazza' had illuminized English soccer and he had been a pretty big part of the success of the English team, rightfully being labelled the Most Valuable Player by the guys on his team.

Although he was having an awesome time in Italy, there was a dark cloud on the horizon for the Londoner. Having already picked up a minor offense card earlier in the tournament, another in that game would mean that he would have to sit out the next match which, if the British had won, would have been the World Soccer Cup final itself.

Sure enough, Gazza picked up another minor OC after a mistimed depossession slide made more contact with the German guy than it did with the soccer ball. As the realization hit him, Gazza started to cry.

Despite being real sad, Gazza dusted himself down and got on with his soccer and the English managed to hold the Germany Westsiders to a tie. Sadly for the Three Lines, they missed out in the deathstrike showdown as the Germans made the final, which they eventually won.

Gazza had entered the tournament not even knowing if he'd play that much soccer. He got off the airplane back in England as a national hero and a soccer player that everybody loved. This would not be the last time he did his soccer in Italy either, as he left the Soccer Chickens for some Italian franchise a year later.

DEPOSSESSION SLIDE !

SOCCERSPEAK...

Depossession slide A skill used in the deefense when you gotta take the soccer ball off an opponent. You slide along that soccer-field floor and kick the soccer ball to safety.

Voluntary simulation plunge (VSP) One of the lamest parts of soccer, where a soccer player throws himself to the floor like he just got hurt but actually just wants a felony kick or the referee to go show their opponent the major felony card. Probably started out in Mexico.

VOLUNTARY SIMULATION PLUNGE!

GRAHAM POLE IS BAD AT MATH

If you attend soccer matches regularly, then you guys probably know what happens when a soccer referee makes a couple of mistakes. Soccer crowds can be brutally honest, and if a referee gets a couple of things wrong, you can expect to hear a typical 'the referee's a dumbass' chant rise up from around the soccer stadium.

As soccer fans, it can also be quite funny when the guy in charge gets something wrong. On this occasion Graham Pole, the British soccer referee, forgot the easiest of soccer sums: one minor offense card + one minor offense card = one major felony card.

Taking charge of a match between the soccer clubs of Australia and Croatia, Pole had already given some Croatian guy a minor offense card. When that same player concedified another felony kick right before the completion whistle, Pole handed out another. Bizarrely, no major felony card followed up.

After eventually blowing the completion whistle, the same Croatian guy got up in Pole's face going crazy at him. Finally, with the math skills of a dumbass kindergarten kid, Pole pulled out a third minor OC, finally followed by the major.

O'CARLOS SCORES A FELONY KICK

>> LYON, FRANCE, 1997

Back in '97, France still had a year to wait before they held the World Soccer Cup of 1998. To help their soccer guys get in shape, they invited Brazil Soccer Club over to the French city of Lyon for an exhibition soccer match.

When the Salsa Boys were given the felony kick way out from the French danger box zone, nobody really expected little Brazilian guy Robert O'Carlos to even attempt to score. Just in case, the French got their deefense formation set up.

O'Carlos was literally real far out, but when he struck the soccer ball with the outside of his left cleat, something more magical than Harry Potter visiting Disney World happened.

Kicked real hard, the soccer ball appeared to be going way far away from the French soccer goal. But as it made its way through the French air, the soccer ball appeared to change its mind and made a swerve toward the soccer goal. With a slight Rick O'Shea off the pipe, it went into the soccer goal interior, going down as one of the most awesome felony kicks ever!

SPECIAL JUAN ANNOUNCES HIMSELF

When Portugaleze franchise Porto made a late equalization goalshot against the Manchester Unity in 2004, soccer fans had no idea who the crazy coach guy running down the soccer field perimeter line was.

Real happy that his franchise were gonna take the win on the aggregation law, this was the moment that most of the soccer world first met Coach Juan Mourinho.

That year was a great one for Juan, as he watched his guys win the Euro Soccer Cup. In London, England, Roman Ibrahimovic clearly liked what he saw and went and hired him as the new Chelsea Franchise Club soccer coach.

In his first press conference, the Portugaleze told the entire world exactly how awesome he was at being a soccer coach:

'I ain't joking, guys, I am real special. I am Special Juan,"

he announced. Special Juan never looked back as his franchise were EPL World Champions in his first two seasons.

5 AWESOME SOCCER COACHES

5 Coach Arsenal Wenger

Despite not winning too many cups lately, the guy with the same name as the franchise at which he has done his better soccer coaching deserves to make it. French and pretty old now, he's taken the Soccer Cannons to the EPL World Championships a whole bunch of times.

4 Coach Alexi Ferguson

Having finally hung up his soccer-coaching boots in 2013, the old Scotch guy was one of the most winningest ever to have coached soccer.

3 Coach Juan Mourinho

The Special Juan has already proven himself to be real great at coaching soccer wherever he has been, and has got more cups than a bra shop.

2 Coach Pip Guardiola

Spanish, this coach totally owned Europe when coaching soccer at Barcelonia, and has already started to do the same at Bryan Munich in EPL Germany.

1 Coach Bruce Arena

Sure, he may sound like a soccer stadium, but he is actually soccer coaching personified. A former goaltender, Bruce has been the main reason behind the success of the LA Galaxy.

THIS IS SOCCER, NOT A HOCKEY MATCH!

>> SANTIAGO, CHILLI, 1962

In soccer, you don't expect to see fights break out; but what happened on the soccer field when Chilli played soccer against Italy Soccer Club in the 1962 World Soccer Cup was a few sticks and helmets short of an NHL hockey match.

After awarding the first felony kick after a few seconds, things escalized real quick. After just 12 minutes, some

CLASSIC SOCCER CHANTS

'You guys ain't singing no more!'

So your franchise was losing, but now they just tied it up. The opposition franchise soccer fans may have been happy before, but they sure ain't now…time to let them know with this great song.

Italian guy got sent back to the locker room by the referee. When he refused, the cops were brought in to take him off the soccer field.

Things did not improve and the soccer match was looking more like a Royal Rumble. It got so bad, that the sports anchor on the BBC in England was forced to introduce a rerun of the match with the following words: 'Hey, there. The match you guys are about to see is the most dumbass, crazy, stupid and disgraceful exhibition of soccer that you will ever see in the history of soccer history.'

It's incredible to think, but before this soccer match was played there was no such thing as minor and major offense cards. Things had gotten so spicy in Chilli that it was in fact the referee in charge that day that patented the idea of minor and major felony cards.

O'BAGGIO'S DEATHSTRIKE FAIL

The World Soccer Cup of 1994 was already a tournament that lit up the world like it was some humongous soccer ball that just got hit by a Fourth of July firework.

The mighty Brazilians had made it all the way through to the final, where they faced the Italians from Italy. Italy Soccer Club's MVP, Robert O'Baggio, had been awesome all soccer tournament and was the main reason they had got to the final—but the guy with a girl's haircut was gonna have the final say for all the wrong reasons on this day in Pasadena.

History remembers this final as 'the final that had everything', and having finished with both sides failing to make the score, a deathstrike showdown eventually decided who would be the World Soccer Cup World Champions of the World, 1994.

After the first deathstrike failed for the Salsa Boys, their other three all made it into the SGI. The same could not be said for the Italians. Their first and fourth were fails, which basically meant that O'Baggio had to insert his to keep them in with a shot of glory.

The pony-tailed soccer player stepped up to the deathstrike plate—surely he was gonna score?

Unfortunately for the nation of pizza lovers, O'Baggio's kick was way too hard and went so high it nearly landed in Texas.

It's been said lots through the years, but here was another example of how soccer can be real cruel. It had been a close shave for the Brazilians, who had been given the victory thanks to one bad kick from one of the best soccer players of that time.

BEST EURO FRANCHISES

PSV

Along with Disney and that real big tower, Paris can now add 'a soccer franchise' to its list of cool things. Traditionally pretty bad at soccer, PSV are a franchise that has benefited from some real rich guys spending some money on them.

TOP 5 VOLUNTARY SIMULATION PLUNGES

5 Jurgen Klinsmann

Before being coach of the USMNT, Coach Klinsmann was German. He even played for them, too. In the 1990 World Soccer Cup Final against Argentina Soccer Club, he fell over like he got hurt real bad.

This resulted in the deefense guy getting the major FC. The Argentines, well known for being totally fair on the soccer field and never attempting to cheat, were pretty mad when they went on to lose 1-0.

Coach Klinsmann still denies the VSP to this day, pointing out that if there was no contact then he wouldn't have got his leg hurt so bad that it needed a Band-Aid.

4 Brian Carassco

If you switch around a couple of letters in this guy's first name, you get the word 'brain', but after what he did when playing soccer for the Chilli Under 20 team, maybe it's clear he didn't have one.

Acting like a total asshat, TV cameras picked him up grabbing a hold of his opponent's arm and pulling it towards his face. He then threw himself to the ground as if he just got hit in the face. Incredibly, the soccer referee gave him the felony kick!

>>

Love them or hate them, VSPs sure are part of the modern game, and here are some of the most talked-about VSP incidents ever.

3 Didier Dogbra

Despite being an awesome, powerful, strong guy, Didier Dogbra spent more time on the ground in his time at Chelsea Franchise Club than a homeless guy with no legs.

When he got kicked by some guy's elbow in a Euro Soccer Cup game, he went down holding his face. Already lame enough, Dogbra was seen taking a sneak peek at what was happening.

2 Sergio Bisquets

When playing for Barcelonia against Italian Milan in 2010, Bisquets fell to the floor. Rolling around like a complete joke, he took a minute to peek at his opponent, who he made out had just hit him in the face. His VSP worked, as the other guy got the major felony card.

>>>

1 Monty Gamst Pederson

In a game against London Arsenal, Pedersen did one of the lamest VSPs on record. Playing for Blackburn Roosters, the Dutchman chased the soccer ball as it went outta play. With a check over his shoulder to see the Soccer Cannon deefense guy behind him, Pederson fell to the floor in anticipization of a deathstrike. To make things worse, Pederson went on to start whining at the soccer referee.

LANDON DONOVAN WEARS A SPORTS BRA

39

Through the years, soccer has always provided us with its fair share of personalities, and nothing screams out 'soccer comedian' more than the name Landon Donovan. Aside from having one of the most decorated soccer careers of the modern era, Landon is well known for being one of the sport's funny guys.

Nothing illustrates this more than the All Stars soccer match back in 2001. When Jim Rooney ripped off his soccer jersey to celebrate a goalshot, he showed off a black sports bra to the millions watching around the globe. Copying the celebration of USA women's soccer player Brandi Chastain, this was dedicated to their favourite female athlete.

Landon Donovan, on the opposing franchise, was not to be outdone. When he tied up the soccer match in the 92nd minute, he too took off his jersey to reveal a black sports bra.

With the soccer world at his cleats, it was a moment that really stood out. Here was a guy that obviously had the talent to go all the way in the sport, yet he still could take a time out from all the serious stuff to show a great sense of humor.

ESPÍNDOLA IN FOOT FRACTURE FELONY

If the MLS handed out an award for soccer douche of the year, Real Salt Lake's Fabián Espíndola would have been front of the queue after what happened this one time in LA back in 2008.

With the eyes of the soccer world fixed upon this corner of Los Angeles for the clash of these two Major League Soccer heavyweights, Espíndola ran away in delight as he put that soccer ball into the Galaxy's net. Celebrating with his trademark flip that he would do every time he scored a goalshot, the soccer player landed, pulled up and started reaching for his foot. He was hurt pretty bad, and would face a spell in the gym.

Already feeling a bit of a douche, things got worse when it turned out the goalshot he'd just called had been rejected by an erected denial flag.

Promising never to do the celebration again, it was a few months before Espíndola returned to a soccer field.

SCORPION HAND DENIAL

Who would be a goaltender, huh? So often the fall guy when it comes to soccer, one night in London, England, one goaltender showed that sometimes the guy between the pipes can be the hero, as he made one of the most incredible hand denials of all time.

Visiting the Wembley Arena that night was Colombia Soccer Club, still recovering from their 2 to 1 thrashing by the USMNT the previous summer.

When the soccer ball found itself at the cleats of Harry Redknapp, he kicked it toward the soccer goal. From real far away, the shot was powerful but not that great, to be honest. Higuita, the Colombian goaltender, started to ready himself for a moment of magic.

Jumping real high into the air, it looked like he was just doing some lame-ass flip. As his feet came over the back of his head his heels kicked the soccer ball away and outta the danger box zone. The hand denial was named the Scorpion kick because of the way Higuita's body shape looked like one of those bugs you get in the desert.

SCHUMACHER KOs A FRENCH GUY

Soccer and wrestling are not two sports that go hand in hand, but soccer fans could have been forgiven for thinking they were watching the WWF if they tuned in to the World Soccer Cup semi-final of 1982.

Knotted at ones, French MVP Mikey Platini played in one of his buddies to take a strike. As he got to the edge of the danger box zone, the Germany goaltender came out to make the gather. Too bad for him, Battistown, the French guy, was pretty quick and got to the soccer ball first. As he kicked it, the ball went outta play, but Schumacher (German for cleat-maker) smashed into his opponent's French face.

Incredibly, the referee did not punish this felony and Schumacher got the soccer ball and got ready for the re-entry kick. Not dead, but it was clear that his opponent was hurt pretty bad—so bad that he left the soccer field with the medics and headed for the hospital.

The Germany Westsiders were eventually the winningest team that day, with Schumacher's hand denials in the deathstrike showdown enough to send the French guys back to France. But this soccer match would be remembered by a lotta soccer fans for this one body slam.

Denial flag erection A flag that can get waved by the soccer referee's helper. This signifies when a goalshot should be denied.

TOP 5 USA SOCCER LEGENDS

5 Freddy Adu

Fresh out of diapers, a real young version of this guy took the MLS by storm and had soccer-loving heads turning all over the place to take a look at him. He has gone on to do soccer right the way around the globe.

4 Clint Dempsey

One of the game's global megastars, Clint Dempsey took the EPL League by storm when playing for Full Ham and eventually got a move to London when he played for Totten Ham Whitespurs. After a year for the Soccer Chickens, Dempsey broke British hearts when he moved back to the MLS with the Seattle Sounders.

>>

3 Brad Friedel

Real old Brad Friedel has been a shining light for goaltenders across Planet Soccer for many years. Like some real ugly kid who nobody wants, Brad Friedel has been passed around from one EPL franchise to another, but that's not to say that nobody wants *him*. He remains one of the winningest goaltenders in the game and is renowned for his awesome hand denials.

2 Landon Donovan

After playing soccer in Germany and England, Landon Donovan's time with the LA Galaxy has earned him a reputation for being a 'one-franchise guy'. An MLS legend, even the arrival of David Beckham to Los Angeles could not keep Landon in the shade. In fact, more soccer fans started to turn out to LA Galaxy games after Beckham started playing for them just to support Landon Donovan.

1 Alexi Lalas

A guy with a head of hair that looked like the flames of soccer passion that burn in his heart, Alexi Lalas was one of the icons of the sport in the 1990s. As well as soccer, his musical ability stood out too. He was the player that personified the World Soccer Cup of 1994 and is widely recognized as one of the faces of the game long after he hung up his cleats.

>>>>>>>>>>>>>>>>>>>>>>>>>>>>>>>>>

AGWEAROOOOOOOOO OOOOOOOOOOOOOOO

Abraham Lincoln once said, 'Never, never, never give up.'

That was pretty much the motto of Coach Ferguson and his Manchester Unity franchise as they became the winningest of all the EPL franchises over the time the Scotchman was there. But in May 2012, the guys from a few blocks away were about to show that they subscribed to Lincoln's words of wisdom.

After a 6 to 1 demolition derby earlier in the soccer season, the Manchester Unity had recovered and looked like they would retainify their World Championship again that year. The 'real loud neighbors', as Coach Ferguson would say, had other ideas. The Unity got their asses beat by the Wigan Athletes and the Sky Blues again, meaning that in their final soccer match of the season Manchester City Franchise Club could go win that League Cup.

At the soccer unleashment whistle, Coach Mankini and his soccer players knew that a victory would be enough against Queens Power Rangers, a franchise who were trying to avoid being relegationized from the EPL.

Things did not go that great though for the blue-uniformed soccer machine. As the overtime verdict board was erected, they were down 2 to 1. The Unity had already won their soccer match someplace else, which meant that only victory points would be enough to get that party started.

Surely they had messed up. Even their own soccer fans were pretty mad with them, and chants of 'You guys suck at soccer,' were clearly heard drifting through the Manchester air.

Then, outta nowhere, a Heading Dzeko headkick tied it all up. Suddenly, at twos, the City guys knew they just needed one more goalshot.

When the Queens Power Rangers made the possession concession after the restart, a tsunami of soccer wetness rushed toward the away franchise's DBZ. As Mario Buyatelly fed the pass-kick to Agwearo, the little guy kicked the soccer ball past the goaltender. It was totally off the hook.

Just as Manchester Unity had started their own party, the 'real loud neighbors' got a whole lot louder.

DENIAL-FLAG HEARTACHE FOR USMNT

Denied goalshots have punctuated the words of the story of soccer right the way through, and what happened to the USMNT in 2010 was perhaps the biggest of periods.

After fighting back from 2 down against a very strong Slovenia soccer team, the Americans were denied a slice of World Soccer Cup history in a real cruel way: Landon Donovan's felony kick was passed into the center of the DBZ where Maurice Edu inserted a no-bounce kick. It was a beautiful goalshot, and would have completed one of the most memorable score flip reversals ever. But it was not to be.

The soccer referee (in his home country of Africa) denied the goalshot and awarded the felony kick for the Slovenia deefense. The reason for the denial was pretty much unclear, and the moment went down in history as probably *the* most controversial goalshot that the soccer world has ever seen.

Fortunately, it did not stop the USMNT from making it to the next stage of the World Soccer Cup.

FREDDY ADU HAS A TRYOUT FOR THE UNITY

>> MANCHESTER, ENGLAND, 2006

Undoubtedly the biggest headline-maker in the world of soccer recently, it was no great surprise when American teen Freddy Adu got asked to a tryout at one of the world's most winningest franchises, the Manchester Unity, back in 2006.

With the likes of Dwayne Rooney and Cristiarnold Ronaldo on their roster, Coach Ferguson clearly dreamed of pairing Adu with the other two guys to make an even more deadly offense than the lethal one that already existed in Manchester.

Although they were probably impressed by Adu's soccering ability, no reason was ever given as to why he never ended up being a full-time Soccer Devil. Eventually, he ended up going someplace else in EPL Portugal and has never looked back, doing soccer in France, Greece, Turkey and Brazil, as well as back in the MLS.

Many believe that the Unity's failure to tie down Adu was the reason for Ronaldo's departure a few years later.

Coach Ferguson could only look on and think what could have been if he had not let Adu slip through his old Scotch fingers.

TOP 5 NO-BOUNCE KICKS OF ALL TIME

5 Zidanine Zidane
After a Robert O'Carlos cross-pass got lobbed to the perimeter of the danger box zone, the French guy's left cleat committed soccer homicide on the ball and sent it into the top of the Bayer Neverleusen net. This strike handed the Euro Soccer Cup back to Real Madrid Franchise Club.

>>>

4 Paolo Di Caprio
After a real big kick drifted over the Wimbledon Crazy Guy's deefense line, the bad-ass Italian cycled it into the score net.

>>>>>>>>>>>>>>>>>>>>>>>>>>>>>>>

3 Toby Yeahboya
Kicking it real hard, Yeahboya's shot Rick O'Shead down off the crosspipe and bounced into the SGI. It was one of the highlights of Leeds Union's EPL life.

The no-bounce kick is one of the most challengingest skills in soccer—and it sure is a great moment when one of these winds up in the Soccer Goal Interior. Here's five of the best.

2 Van Basten

A Neverlands cross-pass was kicked way too high to trouble the opposition deefense…or so it seemed. At the far side of the DBZ, Van Basten arrived and kicked it back across the face of the soccer goal. Soccer fans right around the world went crazy as young Van inserted it from a cute angle.

1 Benny Feilhaber

Sure, the rest of the goalshots on this list have been impressive, but it takes special players to insert them on the biggest of stages. Those stages don't get no bigger than the Gold Cup, and after the Mexican deefense failed to evacuate their danger box that day in 2007, Feilhaber made them pay big time and etched his name into soccer history for all of history.

RAMOS DROPS A SOCCER CUP

After just winning a Soccer Cup against Barcelonia, their long-time haters, this was a great night for the Real Madrid soccer franchise and all their fans.

Hitching a ride through the Madrid streets on some kind of cabriolet bus, the soccer players were in party mood, and so were the guys that had turned out to see them. On top of that bus of soccer joy, the soccer players showed off their big shiny Cup, passing it from one guy to the next—eventually it made its way to Sergio Ramos, and the deefense guy went and dropped the Cup off the bus. The wheels of the bus went right over it, to the horror of everyone watching. The bus and partying stopped. Children cried. The Spanish streets emptied as people went home.

The Cup that the guys from the San Diego Bernabowl had soccered so hard to win now looked like it had been run over by a bus. Sergio Ramos looked like a total jerk.

THE CRAZY GUYS WIN THE ENGLAND SOCCER CUP

47

Think 'Wimbledon' and I betcha you guys think of Pete Sampras, right? Well, back in the day, it wasn't just about tennis bats in this corner of London, England.

In the year 1988, Wimbledon Crazy Guys were a franchise that made it all the way to the Franchise Association Soccer Cup final at Wembley Arena. Unfortunately, the Crazy Guys would face off against Liver Pool—at the peak of their powers.

When some guy called Sanchez (probably Mexican) gave the Wimbledon franchise an early lead, things were looking up. Being one goalshot up, they knew that if their deefense could make the shutout and deny the Mercytown franchise, they would more than likely win this soccer match.

Incredibly, that was exactly what happened. Wave after wave of offensive play was denied by the Crazy Guys as they hung on to cause one of the biggest soccer shockers ever.

Unfortunately for the fans of the Crazy Guys, the good times faded after they ended up relegationized from the EPL League a few years later. After that, the franchise—as they do from time to time—upped and went someplace else.

GEOFF HURTS 'SCORES' A GOALSHOT

48

In soccer, what goes around comes around. When English soccer player Frank Lamphard thought he'd tied up the soccer match with Germany in 2010, the English were pretty mad when they saw that the soccer match continued. After hitting the top pipe, the soccer ball bounced down and clearly into the soccer goal interior. The denial was costly, as the English guys got beat real bad.

The Germans did not feel that bad, however.

Back in the summer of '69, the English had beaten the Germany Westsiders to take their only World Soccer Cup Cup back home to England. Winning 4 to 2, the match MVP was clearly their main inserter of goalshots, Geoff Hurts, who had kicked a triple of goalshots into what his countrymen famously call the 'ball-bag'.

One of them, the third, is still contestified by the guys from Germany to this day. Just like the Lamphard strike in 2010, the soccer ball bounced down after hitting the top pipe. When the soccer ball hit the deck, the English celebrated. It was not clear if the soccer ball had even entered the SGI, so a confused soccer referee went over to the denial-flag erector. After a quick talk, the goalshot was signalized, much to the anger of Germany.

Even after watching instant replays, it's pretty tough to call whether that soccer ball was a genuine goalshot. As much as Hurts hurt the Germans that day, what happened in 2010 may just have tied things up a little.

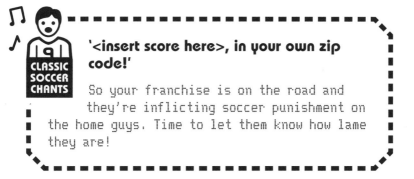

'<insert score here>, in your own zip code!'

So your franchise is on the road and they're inflicting soccer punishment on the home guys. Time to let them know how lame they are!

KUWAIT HERE A MINUTE, GUYS

>> VALLADOLID, SPAIN, 1982

Apart from getting invaded by Saddam Hussein, the only other time people probably heard of Kuwait in the twentieth century was an incident that happened during the 1982 World Soccer Cup in Spain.

Playing France Soccer Club, the Kuwaitish were always gonna get their butts kicked. They had done pretty good to keep the score at 3 to 1 when the French managed to penetrate their deefense for a controversial number four.

Up in the audience, Sheikh Al-Sabah (the owner of Kuwait) was so mad. Even though Kuwait had no chance of even making a tie, the real mad guy ordered that his soccer players exited the soccer field for an illegal time-out and went crazy at the soccer referee until he denied the goalshot.

Eventually, Al got his way, and the soccer match restarted again with the score back at 3 to 1. The French guys eventually did get goalshot number four, leaving the Kuwaitish owner looking a complete soccer douche.

TOP 5 AMERICAN GOALSHOT INSERTERS

5 Joe-Max Moore
Lethal on the international scene, Moore was the face of soccer in the early 00s and enjoyed giving deefenses in Germany and England nightmares at franchise level in a truly unique soccer career.

4 Brian McBride
Lethal on the international scene, McBride was the face of soccer in the early 00s and enjoyed giving deefenses in Germany and England nightmares at franchise level in a truly unique soccer career.

3 Eric Wynalda
Slotting in at three is Eric Wynalda. Impressive on the international scene, Wynalda was a loyal soccer player at franchise level, representing ten different franchises before finally hanging up his cleats.

2 Clint Dempsey
A national hero in America and England, Clint sits in number two in the list of all-time USMNT goalshot inserters.

1 Landon Donovan
If you could translate 'Landon Donovan' into the language of 'soccer' on Google Translate, it would literally mean 'goalshot inserter'. The greatest of all American scorers.

ZICO GOALSHOT DENIED BY THE COMPLETION WHISTLE

Some things in soccer never change, no matter how many years pass on by. The best example of this is a soccer referee's ability to always be the guy that people are hatin' on.

At the end of a soccer match between Sweden and Brazil, the Salsa Boys had a totally legit reason to get crazy with the soccer referee.

Having kicked the corner cross-pass, Brazilian MVP Zico got the headkick to send the soccer ball into the Swedish soccer goal. Deep in overtime, this would have guaranteed victory points for the Brazil guys—but thanks to the referee from Whales, England, it was not to be.

When the cross-pass was airborne, the soccer referee ended the match with the completion whistle. It was a pretty dumb thing to do and was greeted by a bunch of protests from Brazil's soccer players, who got up in the referee's face, hollering at him and going all crazy. With the tie point in the bag, the Swedes breathed a supersized breath of relief.

COMPLETION
★ ★ ★ ★ ★ ★ ★ ★ ★ ★ ★
WHISTLE!

SOCCERSPEAK...

Completion whistle At the end of the soccer match, the referee will blow his whistle and everyone can head back to the locker room.

First published in the United Kingdom in 2014 by
Portico
1 Gower Street
London
WC1E 6HD

An imprint of Pavilion Books Company Limited

ISBN 978-1-90939-673-9

A CIP catalogue record for this book is available from
the British Library.

10 9 8 7 6 5 4 3 2 1

Printed and bound by L.E.G.O. SpA, Italy
This book can be ordered direct from the publisher at
www.pavilionbooks.com

Illustrations by Willie Ryan

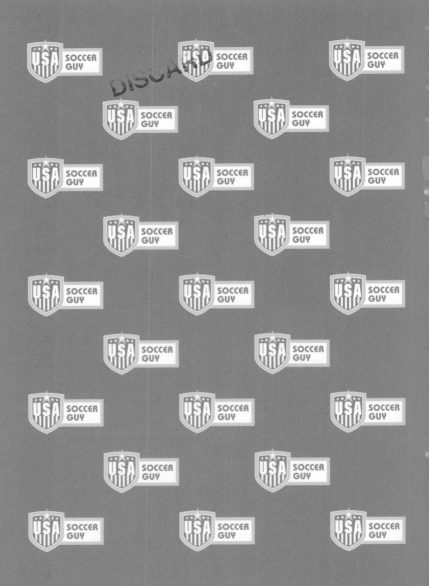